HOW TO READ A COMIC BOOK

Comic books are made up of pictures in boxes, called panels. Look at each of these panels from left to right, and top to bottom.

Read the speech bubbles, caption boxes and any sound effects from left to right, too. Together with the images, these will tell you the story.

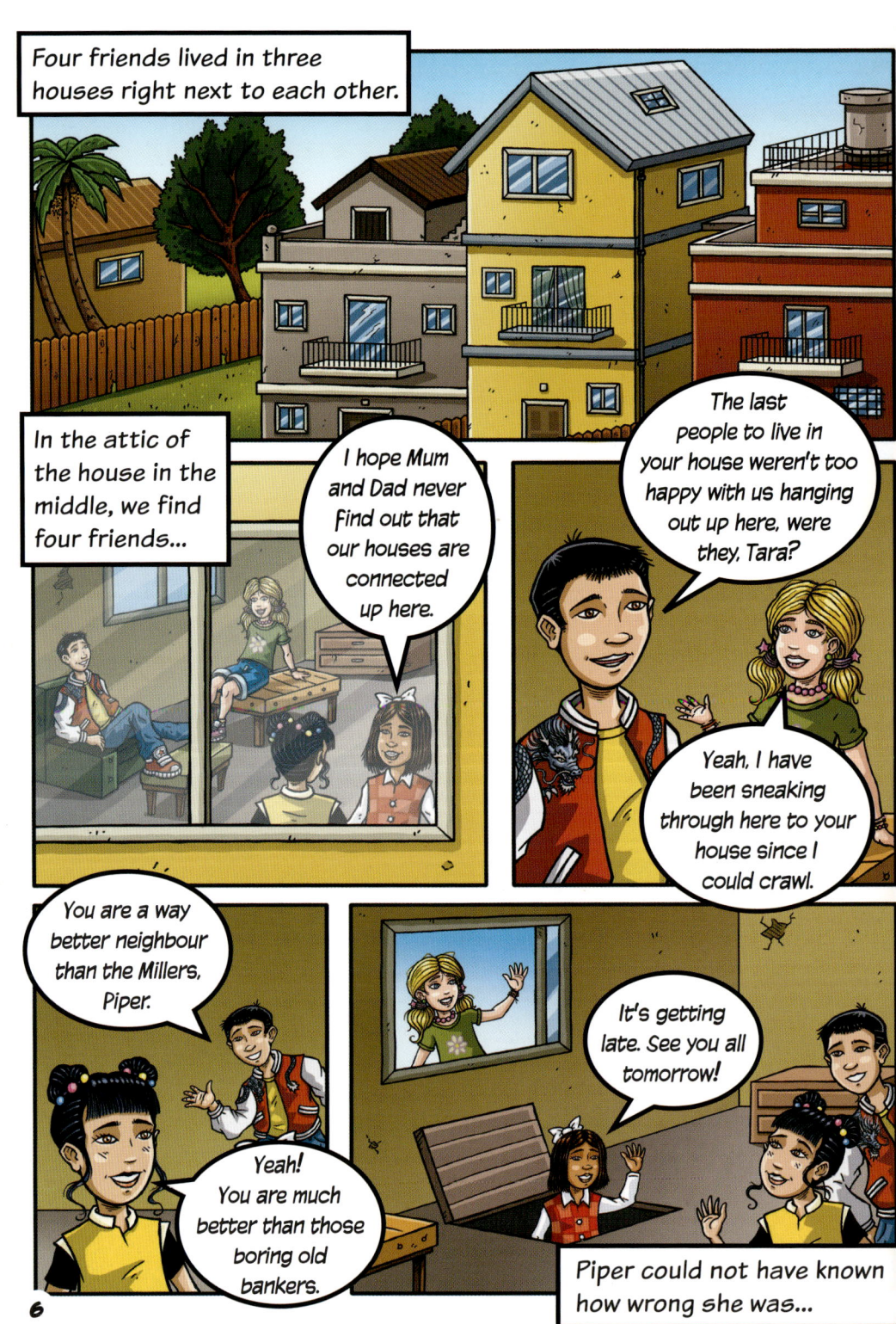

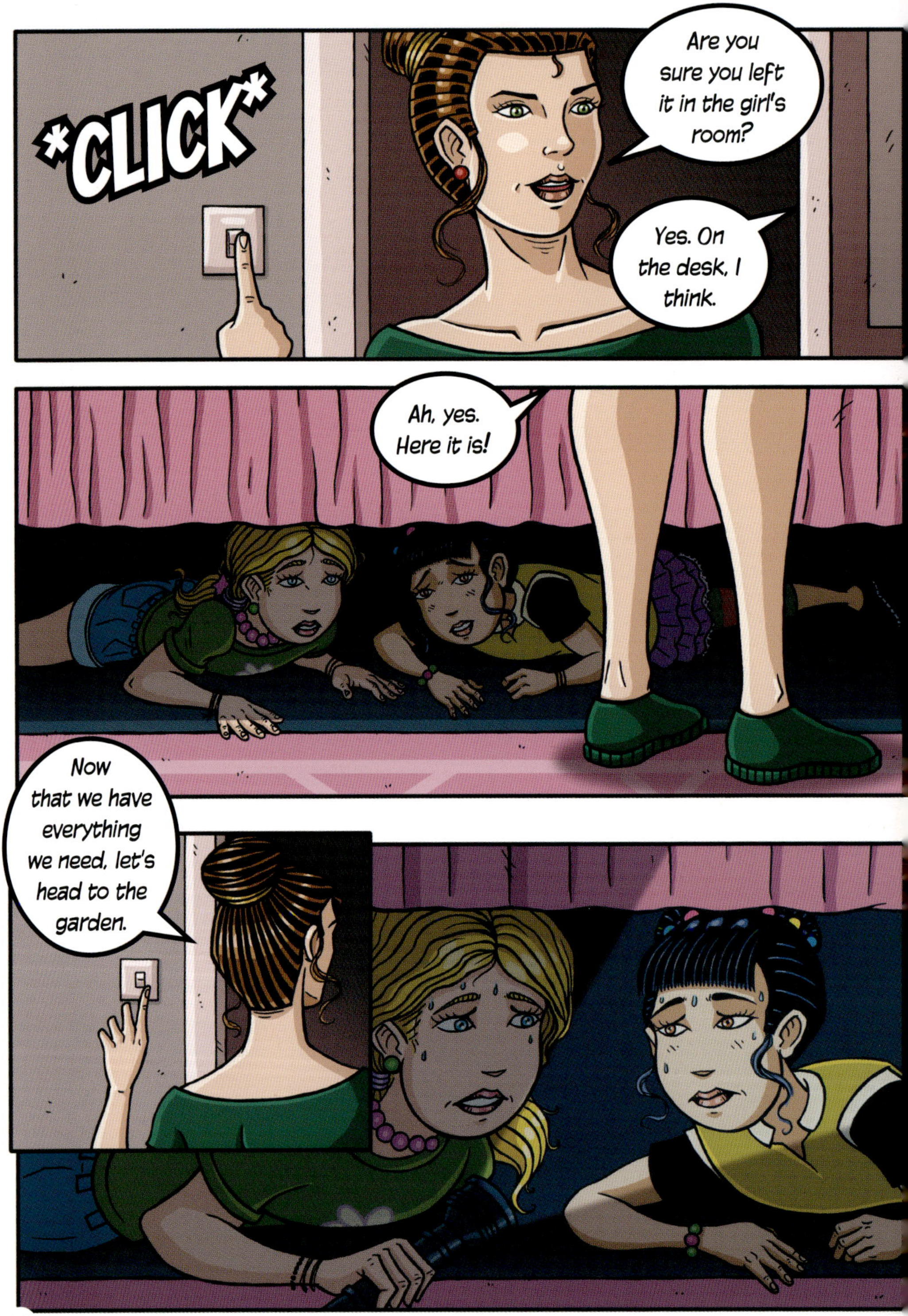

A strange and distant chanting filled the air around them.

It got louder as the girls crept into Piper's parents' room.

The chanting was coming from...

... outside!

@2023 BookLife Publishing Ltd.
King's Lynn, Norfolk, PE30 4LS, UK

ISBN 978-1-80505-046-9

All rights reserved. Printed in China.
A catalogue record for this book is
available from the British Library.

The House in the Middle
Written by Hermione Redshaw
Illustrated by Jaime Espinar Muñoz

ABOUT BOOKLIFE GRAPHIC READERS

BookLife Graphic Readers are designed to encourage reluctant readers to take the next step in their reading adventure. These books are a perfect accompaniment to the BookLife Readers phonics scheme and are designed to be read by children who have a good grasp on reading but are reluctant to pick up a full-prose book. Graphic Readers combine graphic and prose storytelling in a way that aids comprehension and presents a more accessible reading experience for reluctant readers and lovers of comic books.

ABOUT THE AUTHOR

Hermione Redshaw has been writing books for over eight years, with a passion for adventure and fantasy. Her writing is often distinguished by themes of family and personal growth. Hermione holds a Bachelor's degree in English Language, Communication and Linguistics. She has a keen interest in communicating difficult ideas in a clear and accessible way.

ABOUT THE ILLUSTRATOR

Jamie Espinar Muñoz's love for art was passed down to him as part of his family heritage. He is the son, grandson and brother of artists. Jamie studied Fine Arts in college and has extensive experience creating art in a variety of mediums and for different projects, including painting scenery for theatre and television. He has been producing custom illustrations since 2005, working in advertising, magazines, online media and publishing. Now, Jamie is focused on creating illustrations for children's books, comics and even games. He currently resides in Spain with his wife, who works as a graphic designer, his son and their two cats.